Before Your Very Eyes

A Modern Melodrama

by

John Challen

HEINEMANN EDUCATIONAL
BOOKS LTD · LONDON

Heinemann Educational Books Ltd
LONDON EDINBURGH MELBOURNE
SINGAPORE JOHANNESBURG
AUCKLAND IBADAN NEW DELHI
HONG KONG NAIROBI

ISBN 0 435 23160 X

Published by
Heinemann Educational Books Ltd
48 Charles Street, London WIX 8AH
Printed in Great Britain by
Cox & Wyman Ltd
London, Fakenham and Reading

INTRODUCTION

This play was written as a piece of fun, and a considerable part of the fun arises from juxtaposing the standard melodramatic situations and conventions with our own contemporary background and surroundings. For the children for whom the play was written, this meant Crawley but, as you read the play and later, perhaps, perform it, you should replace the Crawley allusions with ones which are relevant to your own area – not only in straightforward ways like changing the name of the town, the local newspaper and so on, but in other ways; you may find a much funnier place for the 'centre of real power', a more relevant password for the spies, more apposite activities for cloaking the start of a World Revolution than a student rag. And so on. The point is, the play enabled us to make a number of light-hearted comments about our community and it needs translating if it is to do the same for yours.

The setting is of a stage within a stage. In our production, we put up a not very large representation of a Victorian stage, using Dexion framework, some old red velvet curtains and tinselly ornamentation. The floor of this 'stage' was made from portable blocks, so it was raised a little above the rest of the acting area which, for us, was simply an open platform. Thus, the melodramatic characters could make their entrance on the 'stage' and then move into the rest of the acting area as required. According to circumstances, that acting area could be quite featureless (ours was, deliberately) or could in some way represent the community. At one point, we thought of decorating our area with road signs, particularly 'No Entry' and other prohibiting ones, but we decided that this could be confusing. The setting, as such, we confined to the 'stage' and the scene painters had great fun thinly disguising local settings by representing them in pantomime-style backcloths which, being at the back of the inner 'stage' were thus kept to manageable proportions while still serving, quite validly, to set the scene. We selected those scenes we wanted to 'set'; we didn't, in fact, set them all. The Chairman's rostrum and desk were placed right at the front of the acting area, Down Left, so that he could be seen to be introducing, not only action on the 'stage', but also that on the acting area.

Music: basically, the Gang's music was live and the Villain's, canned. We had a small group: piano, guitars, drums. Any sort of live music could be appropriate, but a piano is, I feel, pretty essential. We surrounded our group with potted palms and they were quite decorative. For the Villain, we used dramatic music – some would say melodramatic. Certainly, we used a lot of Wagner, some Suppé, some Gounod. The solemn, live, music tended to be 'Land of Hope and Glory', that being a piece which the pianist could play, and throughout we used what was appropriate or suggested – or happened to be available. We couldn't get the Gang to sing 'For he is an Englishman' so we settled for 'Rule Britannia'.

The play was written for a group of youngsters with tremendous verve and zest and that is really what it needs in performance – attack and an ability to make the most out of any situation. The Chairman's speeches, for example, were far better than those set down here – he played them off the cuff and got excellent audience response. The rest of the cast, too, developed the situations according to their inclinations and talents – the Dancers and Witches devised their own routines; the Gang and the Villain, their 'silent film' episode, and so on. A group of gymnasts produced an excellent sequence, as 'thugs' in training, which appeared marginally more perilous than in fact it was, so we introduced it before the knitting scene, with a few extra lines improvised by the Villain. This is the best way for the production to develop.

At one time, we were going to make some actual silent film sequences on 16 mm and interpolate them into the action – the Knitters bounding through the streets, the Gang searching for Mildred, and so on, but this did not prove practicable. Still, another group might find this fun to do.

The lighting – using a Strand Junior Eight board and mercury vapour spots of the type often used for 'spotlighting' shop-window displays – was simple. With a more elaborate lighting system, we would no doubt have tackled it more elaborately, but the main essential really is to be able to 'localize' lighting, to pick out one part of the acting area while leaving the rest effectively dark. The purpose of the lighting was to keep the action moving swiftly.

In general, the costumes were readily supplied by the children themselves – nothing very elaborate is needed, but there are plenty of opportunities for bright colours and perhaps rather tawdry display. Robert devised his own scalping very effectively with a pale bathing-cap turned inside-out and splodged with 'blood'.

As you will see, there is a large cast; when we did it, we had a hundred or so in it – we never finally got round to counting them. However, it can obviously be done with far less; there are plenty of opportunities for 'doubling'. Use as many children as you feel you can, though. I think they will find the play fun, and if they have fun, they can't help sharing it with the audience.

J.C.

To Keefy and Toby and Andrew and Ian and John and Frank and, of course, Linda and, of course, the villainous Chris and, of course, the alliterative Patrick . . . and, of course, all the rest of you. Thanks.

CHARACTERS

THE CHAIRMAN

KEITH
LUX
ROBERT
GRAHAM } *The Gang*
MILDRED
WILLIAM
PHIL

THE HORSE
GIRLS
1ST SPY; 2ND SPY; GAGGLE OF SPIES
ORIENTAL DANCERS
THE VILLAIN

EMILY
MILLICENT
WINIFRED
AMANDA } *The Knitting Group*
MAUD
JANE
VICTORIA

GAVOTTE DANCERS

HERBERT
PERCY
ELVIRA } *Secret Agents*
MABEL *in disguise*
ICE-CREAM MAN (ALFONSO)
HEAD

SHOPPERS; ADVERTISERS; CHINESE; INJUNS;
TWO INNOCENT CHILDREN

ACT ONE

The setting: a stage within a stage. At the back of the acting area, a reproduction of a Victorian Music Hall stage. (This is referred to as the 'stage'; for more information of the setting, see the Introduction.) At the front of the acting area, a rostrum and desk for the Chairman. After some introductory music, a roll on the drums and a spotlight on the CHAIRMAN. *He should model his approach on the old-type Music Hall.*

CHAIRMAN: Good evening, ladies and gentlemen! And now . . . before your very eyes we present a scintillating, sardonic, supremely satisfying extravaganza, a venturesome, virtuosic vibration of versatile vitality. Now! This very evening! And, on our bill for your delight, delectation and delirious diversion, ladies and gentlemen . . . (*A bang with his hammer.*) . . . A pyrotechnic panorama of prancing pulchritude.

The ORIENTAL DANCERS *make their way across the 'stage', to music, beaming glassily. At the same time, showing no awareness of the action behind them, two of the Gang,* KEITH *and* LUX, *walk mournfully across the front part of the acting area, miserable, bored, hands in pockets of their casual, rather battered, clothes. Heaving deep sighs of boredom, they settle on the opposite side of the stage to the* CHAIRMAN, *who continues.*

CHAIRMAN: And, furthermore: the quintessential quality of equine quadrupeds!

On the 'stage', the PANTOMIME HORSE *appears and cavorts. Meanwhile, two more members of the Gang,* ROBERT *and* GRAHAM, *make their way across in the same way as their companions, who remain sunk in dejection and apathy. The* CHAIRMAN *continues.*

CHAIRMAN: And, for your further dazzled delectation: a soul-stirring simulacrum of a symbolic, super-suspenseful witches' sabbath!

The WITCHES *appear on the 'stage' and, across the acting area, stalks* MILDRED, *Keith's sister, followed by the grimacing pair,* WILLIAM *and* PHIL. *She stands slightly apart from the Gang, while the boys flop down and assume miserable expressions. The* CHAIRMAN *continues, oblivious.*

CHAIRMAN: And a host of other astonishing apparitions – now . . . (*bang with hammer*) this very moment . . . (*bang*) in this very place . . . (*bang*) and, what's more . . . before your very eyes!

The light goes out on him and he retires. Simultaneously, the lights go out on the 'stage' and lights concentrate on the Gang and their acting area. A pause, then they heave a deep, simultaneous sigh, flopping into yet other positions of boredom.

LUX: I mean, it's boring. Crawley's just . . . boring. I mean, what is there to do – I ask you – what is there to do?

KEITH: Could go down the Embassy. It's an all-U programme. (*With relish*) . . . *Lust and the Vampires.*

ROBERT. Oh, very clever. And who's going to pay?

KEITH (*defensive*): Well, it was just a suggestion.

ROBERT (*scathing*): Well, the next time your atomic brain gets struck by a flash of illumination like that, just do us a favour and keep it to yourself.

KEITH (*peevish*): It was a suggestion, I said.

ROBERT: Just a suggestion! Well, just for your information, bird-brain, in the first place that film's so old that I've seen it twice already – on telly, what's more – and, in the second place . . .

GRAHAM: Nobody's got any money.

ROBERT: So there!

KEITH: Well, it was just a suggestion . . .

ROBERT: Oh, shut up!

KEITH: Who are you telling to shut up?

ROBERT: Who do you think?

KEITH (*aggressive*): So.

ROBERT (*provocative*): So?

A pause. The Gang more alert, in anticipation of a fight. KEITH is a little unsure.

KEITH (*spinning it out*): Right.

ROBERT (*provocative*): Right.

KEITH: You want to watch it, I tell you.

ROBERT: Oh. . . .

He produces a lip-bubbling noise of extreme provocativeness combined with a hideous face. KEITH leaps at him and they swirl into a fight. The Gang leaps to life around them.

GRAHAM (*after a suitable interval. Decisive*): That's enough.

LUX takes hold of the two antagonists and holds them apart, still vainly trying to battle with each other. He pursues his theme.

LUX: I mean, nothing ever happens here. It's dead boring.

MILDRED (*nag*): Something'll happen when you get home tonight, Keith, I can tell you. Just look at your trousers – and your shirt. That was clean on this morning. I don't know how you get yourself so filthy. It's beyond me. Just look at you. And tuck your shirt in.

KEITH (*cowed; still held by* LUX, *too*): How can I?

MILDRED: Here, let me —

KEITH (*breaking away*): Oh no, you don't.

MILDRED: And where's your tie? You had one on this morning, I know, because I heard Mum telling you – and just look at your shoes —

KEITH: Oh, give over, do.

WILLIAM: No, she's right, you know. (*He adopts a solemn, oratorical tone, which is underlined by solemn, measured music of rather superficially uplifting nature.*) A man's got to make the most of himself. It's his duty to beautify the world.

ROBERT (*taken aback*): To what?

WILLIAM (*pontificating*): To irradiate the miasmal grey of our existence with the vivid effulgence, the scintillating dynamism —

LUX (*lost*): Eh? Wassat?

MILDRED (*practical*): In other words, why can't you be more like Phil?

   PHIL *is at this moment combing his hair and arranging it into pretty patterns.*

KEITH: What? Like him? Spends all day doing nothing but making himself look beautiful. And where does it get him?

A group of girls, moving across, linger swooningly in PHIL*'s area.*

GIRLS: Hi Phil, Hi Phil . . . oh I think he's gorgeous . . . Hi, Phil . . .

MILDRED: That's where it gets him.

KEITH: So? Who wants a crowd of girls swooning over him?

PHIL (*still combing, not turning*): You'll learn, laddie, you'll learn, give it a year or two . . . you're young yet.

KEITH: Sickening!

WILLIAM (*this speech sets the pattern of slipping into a melodramatic convention: it, too, is backed by noble music and is delivered in the style of an old-fashioned politician*): Ah, no! Never speak disparagingly of your fellows. Albeit, indeed, albeit, there be differences, nay gulfs, between us . . . no man is an island . . . albeit; indeed, forsooth . . . nay, verily . . . and remember this my friends – nay, my comrades – nay, I go further: friends, yes; comrades indeed; but more than that, I venture at this solemn moment in time . . . to address you . . . as mates . . . cobbers. And furthermore, remember this. Always remember. We are not the same as other men. For we . . . we . . . are Englishmen.

They all adopt solemn poses and sing 'For he is an Englishman'. After this, they pause and look at each other, puzzled.

GRAHAM: That's odd. We don't normally burst out into choruses by second-rate English composers. Something must be happening.

B

LUX: Eh? What's that? What's that you say? Something happening? Something actually *happening* in Crawley?

The lights come up on the 'stage' and two palpable villains lurk their way across, moving forward on to the acting area, while the rest of the Gang watch, open-mouthed. LUX, *however, continues, oblivious.*

LUX: I mean, at last – all those years we've waited for Crawley to rise from its slumber in front of the telly and for something – really – to happen!

1ST SPY: Psst!

2ND SPY: Psst!

LUX: Here. who are you saying Psst to?

GANG: Psst!

At last LUX *realizes what is intriguing them. He, too, watches as the* SPIES *continue their heavily melodramatic conversation.*

1ST SPY: Psst!

2ND SPY: Psst!

1ST SPY: You're sure no one can hear us?

2ND SPY (*after a brief glance at the audience*): No one who matters.

1ST SPY: So. Now to call a conference. Listen. (*He blows a whistle. No sound.*)

2ND SPY: I hear nothing.

1ST SPY: Precisely. That is the fiendish ingenuity of it. This is a supersonic whistle, and all our spies have a fiendish oriental device which enables them to pick up the signal and come galloping.

There is a thunderous clatter of hooves as the HORSE *comes clattering across the 'stage' and on to the acting area.*

2ND SPY: Alfonse – look!

1ST SPY: A spy!

2ND SPY: Is he . . . is he . . . one of ours?

1ST SPY: Certainly not! We wouldn't stoop to such depths. (*Savagely to the horse.*) Be off with you, you lick-spittle slave of Fascist overlords!

The HORSE *evinces distinct signs of being hurt.*

2ND SPY: Ah look, you've hurt its feelings!

The HORSE *rolls about, very upset.*

1ST SPY: Good! Now perhaps he'll go away.

The HORSE *continues his antics.*

2ND SPY: Alfonse! This is serious!

1ST SPY: Nonsense, Otto – it's only a horse!

2ND SPY: That's just it – an animal! And, don't forget – you are in England. And, in England – in England, you can commit the most dastardly crime and the newspapers will fight (and pay) for the privilege of publishing your memoirs; you can knock a policeman's helmet off, and they will call it a lark – or a demonstration, which is much the same thing; you can abuse their Prime Minister and they will buy you a drink – but . . . *but* – be cruel to an animal – especially a *horse* – do that, and they'll get right shirty.

1ST SPY: Well, make him go away!

2ND SPY: Perhaps it's a her.

1ST SPY: What difference does that make?

2ND SPY: A lot. If it's a her, she'll hang on just to tease.

1ST SPY: Ah! I have it!

He produces another whistle and blows it. Again, no sound, but the HORSE *evinces great signs of alarm and gallops off.*

2ND SPY: Marvellous! What does that whistle do?

1ST SPY: It produces – ultra-sonically, of course – the

sound made by a Belgian horse-meat dealer. Now, where are those spies?

From all parts of the hall, SPIES *appear, all lurking round and 'histing' one another. The acting area is soon filled with a murmurous gaggle of them, all in picturesque positions.*

1ST SPY: Halt!

They freeze, in dramatic positions.

1ST SPY: Give the password!

SPIES: Rhubarb! (*Murmured, whispered ad nauseam.*)

1ST SPY: That is good. Now, listen. The message must be passed on. One of us has it, but no one must know who. Utmost secrecy must be preserved. But the message must be passed on. In utmost secrecy.

The SPIES *weave in and out in a 'message-passing' sequence. They should present a constantly moving pattern, with pretend messages being passed in all manner of surreptitious ways. After a while, the Gang feel that they should join in this activity and they weave their way into the collection. After a while, the* 1ST SPY *calls out, and all the* SPIES *freeze again, but the Gang move back to their corner,* WILLIAM *carrying, somewhat mystified, a document which he has been passed by one of the Spies.*

1ST SPY: It should have reached me by this time! Who has it? Come! Who has it? I know I said utmost secrecy must be preserved, but that didn't include *me*! I give you one last chance. Whoever has it will call out 'Bingo'. (*Silence.*) It's lost!

The spies all echo 'It's lost' in frantic whispers. Meanwhile, WILLIAM, *with the Gang, has been studying his document.*

WILLIAM: I say – listen to this: Plan to overcome the world —

All the SPIES *turn, horror-struck.*

1ST SPY: All is discovered! We are undone! Woe! Woe! Fly, fly for your lives!

All the SPIES *surge out, all ways. The light gos out on the 'stage' and the scenery is changed.*

WILLIAM: Now what was all that about? Anyway, they've gone, thank goodness. All that *lurking.* Most un-English.

GRAHAM: Just what is that peculiar document you're holding?

WILLIAM: I told you: 'Plan to overcome the world. Section A: most vulnerable spots. Contrary to general beliefs, an area such as Crawley would be relatively easy to overcome. Timing is all-important. On a Saturday afternoon, for instance, an armed take-over would readily be accepted in the belief that it was either a student rag or a detergent advertisement. Still better, one staged during the screening of Coronation Street or Match of the Week would probably not be noticed at all . . .' Gad! The fiendish ingenuity!

KEITH: The diabolical cunning!

ROBERT: The devilish brilliance of it!

LUX: Most un-English.

GRAHAM: But shall they succeed?

ALL: Never!

GRAHAM: No, never! Not while we are here to thwart them!

Resounding patriotic music. They move naturally into a stirring tableau.

PHIL: But how?

GRAHAM: How what?

PHIL: How are we going to thwart them?

GRAHAM: We'll find a way. Never fear.

Again, patriotic music. Again, a noble and impressive tableau.

PHIL: Not if you keep going off into tableaux, you won't. What you want is a bit less pom, pom, pom and a bit more hurry music. There's been too much talking so far. It's a besetting sin of these Lower School productions – too much talk and too little action.

MILDRED: But what action *can* we take? We don't even know where to *start*!

KEITH: We could go to the police —

A general chorus of derision.

ROBERT: Oh yes, I can just see . . . 'please Constable, we've come to report a plot to take over the world, beginning with Crawley . . .'

KEITH: Well, it was a thought.

ROBERT: In your estimation, maybe.

They mount a quick, token fight, but the relish has gone from it.

WILLIAM (*back to the document*): But listen to this: 'It is, therefore, my intention to establish my headquarters in Crawley. Underground, and as close to the centre of real power as possible. The entrance will be concealed under the third paving-stone to the left in front of the Civic Centre. . . .'

LUX: That's it, then, men! To the third paving-stone on the left!

GRAHAM: Onwards! To the third paving-stone on the left!

ALL: To the third paving-stone on the left!

Start of patriotic music and inevitable tableau, but PHIL *breaks in.*

PHIL: No! I've told you once! Let's have a bit of hurry music, or the plot'll never get under way!

To hurry music, they jerk off, in the manner of silent films. The scene is revealed, and they move on again with digging implements – or they could, equally effectively, mime the digging. It is LUX *who is doing the bulk of the work, but all, even* MILDRED, *lend a hand – except* GRAHAM, *who watches their efforts with disdain.*

GRAHAM: Well, get a move on! I don't know – if you went any slower, you'd be in reverse!

LUX (*puffing*): All very well for you to talk!

GRAHAM: Talk about British workmen. Any minute now, they'll stop for tea break – and no one'll notice the difference!

LUX: How about you having a go, then?

GRAHAM: I'm in the executive class. Anyway, it's moving.

MILDRED (*dancing up and down*): It's moving! It's moving! Oh, I'm so excited! What will we find under it, I wonder?

GRAHAM: Solid clay, I expect.

MILDRED: Oh, you are a spoilsport! I think it's so exciting – it's just like a second-rate television programme.

The others have heaved up the paving-stone, or mimed it. GRAHAM *moves to them.*

GRAHAM: Well – what is it?

PHIL: Steps.

GRAHAM: Steps?

PHIL: Steps. Going downward.

GRAHAM: Well, they'd hardly ... anyway, who's going first?

Everyone shows a marked disinclination – they all want someone else to go.

GRAHAM: Well, someone's got to. (*Simultaneously, all heads turn to look at Mildred.*) Gentlemen, the problem's solved. Courtesy demands that pride of place should go to the lady in our midst.

Stirring music, continuing under the following.

GRAHAM: For England!

MILDRED (*carried away*): For England!

ALL: For England!

MILDRED: For the glory of womanhood!

ALL: For the glory of womanhood!

MILDRED and GRAHAM: For Queen and Empire!

ALL: For Queen and Empire!

PHIL: For goodness' sake —

ALL: For goodness' sake ... get on with it!

MILDRED (*the music stops; suddenly dubious*): But I don't want to!

PHIL: You should have thought of that before ... go on!

MURIEL disappears down the hole. They adopt noble poses.

GRAHAM: A noble woman!

ROBERT: Intrepid female!

KEITH: Gallant lass!

WILLIAM: Good riddance!

Whereupon, MILDRED re-appears. They all lean eagerly towards her.

ALL: Well?

MILDRED: I went down the steps —

ALL: Well?

MILDRED: And half-way down —

ALL: Yes?

MILDRED: There's a big notice —

ALL: Yes?

MILDRED: It says —

ALL: Yes?

MILDRED: 'Members Only.'

There is a general despondency. They start to move off.

LUX: Well, that's that, then.

MILDRED: Wait a minute . . . (*They pause.*) I *am* a member. Of the Girl Guides.

GRAHAM: That's true. And I'm a member of Judo Club.

With increasing enthusiasm, they all give their memberships of groups of varying degrees of appropriateness – all except William. They look questioningly at him.

GRAHAM: William?

WILLIAM (*sad; isolated*): It's no use. I'm essentially an individualist.

LUX: Well, that's that, then.

They start to move away from William. Then, suddenly.

WILLIAM: Wait a minute, though! Of course, that's it! I, too, am a member —

ROBERT: What of?

WILLIAM: Of the human race, of course. (*A roll of drums.*) Thank you. Shall we proceed?

They go off. The scene changes, revealing a lush and decadent background. Light is up on the 'stage' as well as the acting area. They troop back on, through the 'stage', looking with awe at the setting, moving back into the acting area.

KEITH: Gosh! It's a Chinese restaurant!

PHIL: Chinese restaurant nothing. It's a Den of Vice.

KEITH: Oh good, I've always wanted to see one of those. (*The others look at him rather dubiously.*) Remember – I am an Englishman – and therefore incorruptible. (*A roll on the drums.*)

GRAHAM: It's a pretty exotic place, anyway.

LUX (*disapproving*): Very un-English.

MILDRED: I can hear music playing.

KEITH: That's just to lower your resistance, like in the shops. What's the betting in a minute they'll try to flog you a new experience in cornflakes.

MILDRED: No – it's real music – live music.

GRAHAM: That's odd.

MILDRED: And, what's more – it's coming from . . . here.

She strides to a door on the side, opens it. A great blast of Wagner. She closes the door and staggers back, much shocked.

MILDRED: Well!

ROBERT: Well, what is it?

MILDRED: They've got the whole of the London Philharmonic Orchestra locked up in there!

KEITH: What? In that little room?

MILDRED: There's two layers – one sitting on the shoulders of the others. It's *very* inconvenient for the lower rows of cellists.

WILLIAM: Gad! It's baffling!

KEITH: A desperately intriguing problem.

GRAHAM: What is it all about?

LUX: Where will it all end?

ROBERT: What is the mystery behind the locked cupboard full of London Philharmonic?

MILDRED: Who can tell?

To the strains of seductive music, the ORIENTAL DANCERS *make their way on to the 'stage'.*

KEITH: I told you – here comes the commercial.

PHIL (*appreciative*): Some commercial!

The dance develops and moves into the acting area. The very glamorous and seductive dancers circle WILLIAM, *who becomes very hot and embarrassed at their admiring attentions. At the end of the dance, the* DANCERS *group seductively round an increasingly hot and bothered* WILLIAM.

WILLIAM: Remember, I am an Englishman, and therefore incorruptible. (*They coo, ingratiatingly.*) Remember that . . . remember it, I say, for I'm in grave danger of forgetting it myself!

KEITH: Steady on, old man. Just bear in mind – a pukka Englishman never fraternizes with the natives. Not done.

WILLIAM: Ah, but the sun is fast setting on the Empire.

KEITH: Nevertheless, it still gives quite enough light for us to see just what you're up to.

WILLIAM: You're right, old man. Not quite the thing, eh?

He walks away from them to receive a firm and manly handshake.

KEITH: Stout fellow.

Whereupon the GIRLS *flock round Phil, making admiring noises.*

WILLIAM (*peeved*): Well, look at him!

PHIL (*smug*): I am an Englishman, and therefore incorruptible.

WILLIAM (*peeved*): That's my line!

PHIL: Not any longer, it isn't. Boy, am I going to enjoy incorruptibility!

Suddenly, impressive music – another roar of Wagner. The DANCING GIRLS *scream and scatter. The others swing towards the Up Centre position. It is an impressive build-up, and, making suitable use of it, the* VILLAIN *strides on to the centre of the 'stage'.*

VILLAIN (*ominous, terrifying*): Aha!

MILDRED: I beg your pardon?

VILLAIN (*peeved*): Aha! Aha!

MILDRED (*unmoved*): I see. And just what's that supposed to mean?

VILLAIN: It's my entrance line. And a very impressive one, too.

MILDRED (*sceptic*): Who says?

VILLAIN (*in fury*): *I* say. And I'm an expert. Look at you. the lot of you. I must say, I don't know what the world's coming to. Youth of today – look at it! Pack of amateurs. Don't recognize professionalism when you see it. Don't know what they teach you in schools nowadays . . . Maths! Waste of time. Science – contemporary superstition. Foreign Languages —

ALL: Ugh!

VILLAIN: Exactly. When what they should be teaching is the essentials – like how to make an entrance. And how to make an exit. Unless you know that, you just can't be a villain.

MILDRED: And who wants to be a villain?

VILLAIN: Everyone, of course. Haven't you noticed how dull the heroes always are? Unless they've got a good splash of villainy in their make-up of course. Oh, I know villainy's not socially acceptable at the moment – it's all right to be devilish cunning, but not plain devilish. That's why we really proficient villains are so successful.

MILDRED (*sudden; accusing*): Why have you got the London Philharmonic shut up in that little room?

VILLAIN: Curses! Me wicked secret's discovered! They've been at the Wagner again, I knew it. It does carry so!

MILDRED: But what have you got them *for*?

VILLAIN. For my entrances, of course. Plus the fact that being associated with music gives any villain a bit of class. But primarily for the entrances.

LUX: The entrances?

VILLAIN: Yes, of course, you stupid object. Just try making an entrance without music – well, go on, try.

They make various attempts, but they are all very feeble and excite the derision of the Dancing Girls. The VILLAIN *watches, triumphant.*

VILLAIN: You see! Whereas, with a good old dollop of your actual classical, cultural, heavily subsidized symphonic malarky – perceive the difference — (*Opening the door.*) Go on, you lot – you can let your tuttis rip, now!

A full-blooded blast of Wagner. To this, the VILLAIN *makes an awe-inspiring entrance. Even the Gang cannot forbear clapping. However, the music continues, unabated, even after the* VILLAIN *has stopped.*

VILLAIN: That's enough! That's enough! That's the trouble with these musical types; give them a semibreve and they take an appoggiatura. Quiet, dogs! Else you'll be on bread and water for a week – or the Messiah, which would be even worse!

Groans; the music stops abruptly.

WILLIAM (*shocked*): You villain!

VILLAIN: Yes, that's what I am. An out-and-out-dyed-in-the-wool villain. And proud of it. (*Hisses.*) Hiss away! I bet you wish you could change the colour of your face at will. (*It changes to bright green and continues to change during the rest of the speech.*) But I can! Because I'm a successful rotter! (*Boos.*) Boo all you like! Boos are the breath of life to me – because I'm unashamed in my rank villainy – so there! And I know full well why you boo – it's not disapproval – it's envy – oh yes it is! Because I'm a full-time villain with the courage of his convictions. I gain positive pleasure from turning a helpless widow out of house and home into a blizzard – whereas you . . . you parttimers, you amateurs – all you can manage is to swipe a few sheets of blotting-paper at the office – kid's stuff – or get off the bus without paying your fare – feeble – or make your neighbours' life an absolute misery – pathetic – or wangle your income tax – I ask you! You ought to be ashamed of yourselves! Your pathetic little bits of villainy are just not worth the effort; whereas I . . . *I* – am a villain on the sort of scale you'd like to be – if only you had the courage! (*Boos.*) And boo to you, too! I shall take over the whole world —

WILLIAM: Starting with Crawley, you cur!

VILLAIN (*conversational*): That's right. But how did you know?

WILLIAM: See, we have your plans. All is discovered?

VILLAIN: No matter. You are too late. Nothing can stop me now. I have it all worked out. And in half an hour precisely, I shall start to take over the world. The whole world! Hee! Hee! The whole world! (*He cackles insanely.*)

LUX: Half an hour! Then there's no time to lose, if this foul fiend's plan is to be foiled! Hurry, men!

GRAHAM: Make haste, chaps!

PHIL: Where?

GRAHAM: I beg your pardon?

PHIL: Where are we making haste to?

GRAHAM: That's a point. Er, excuse me – just where is the armed uprising going to take place?

VILLAIN: Ho! Ho! Armed uprising! Oh, ho, ho, ho! (*He cackles maniacally and his face changes colour surprisingly.*)

LUX: He'll do himself an injury if he keeps changing colour like that.

MILDRED: You mean – there isn't going to be an armed uprising?

VILLAIN: Certainly not – it's not necessary. All the preliminary work is done. I have infiltrated every group and society in Crawley. That was all I had to do. And, when the revolution comes, in precisely . . . twenty-seven minutes, it will be eminently *respectable*. In this country, people will accept anything, so long as you make it look respectable. Launch it with an armed uprising? Oh dear me, no – I shall launch my revolution with a wine and cheese party.

KEITH (*aghast*): Egad! The fiendish cunning of it! The English will accept *anything* that's launched with a wine and cheese party. Is there no end to this fiend's devilment?

Solemn music. The Gang move to the front of the stage, adopting solemn poses.

GRAHAM: The lamps are going out all over Crawley.

ROBERT: Is this an end to civilization as we have known it?

MILDRED: Is it an end to fish and chips and off-licences?

LUX: To Bingo and Come Dancing?

KEITH: To transistor radios and litter?

PHIL: Farewell, farewell, the fivepenny post —

WILLIAM: To seaside rock, to public opinion polls, to plastic cups and flowers, a long and lasting farewell.

LUX: Where will it end, ah where will it end?

Tableau. But suddenly MILDRED *speaks. The music stops, the mood changes.*

MILDRED: Anyway, I bet there's one group you haven't infiltrated, because my Aunt Maisie's in it, and I'd have heard if you had.

VILLAIN: I have infiltrated them all. Nothing can stop me now.

MILDRED: You're wrong, I bet. What about Aunt Maisie's group – the Tilgate Women's Knitting and Friendly Group?

VILLAIN (*twitching spasmodically*): Ha! Clever. Very clever. But not clever enough. True, I found those women a problem. Too incorruptible by half.

MILDRED: I told you so!

VILLAIN: Ha! You rejoice too soon! I couldn't nobble them, true. So, I nobbled . . . their knitting-needles!

WILLIAM: You unmitigated cur! Are not even knitting-needles safe from your villainy? Are there no depths to which you will not sink?

VILLAIN: Frankly, no.

GRAHAM: Don't boast too soon. We will thwart your evil designs.

VILLAIN: Don't kid yourselves. Just as soon as they handle those impregnated atomic knitting-needles, their characters will undergo a remarkable transformation.

MILDRED: For the sake of knitting circles throughout this plain and purl kingdom – his evil plans must not prevail! (*Fanfare.*) To the Tilgate Women's Knitting and Friendly Circle!

ALL (*tableau*): To the Tilgate Women's Knitting and Friendly Circle!

They gallop off.

VILLAIN: Too late, by me beard and britches, too late! Now then, you lot, earn your keep – you're not just here to look ornamental, you know.

The ORIENTAL DANCERS *start to set the next scene as the* VILLAIN *goes off. The 'stage' and acting area are in relative darkness; spotlight on the* CHAIRMAN.

CHAIRMAN: And now, ladies and gentlemen, from the exotic purlieus of international vice to yet another sensational scene, never before revealed on any stage. Indeed, it is only because the Lord Chamberlain is no longer in business that we are able to reveal to you in frank, fearless and unashamed realism just what goes on behind the closed doors of a certain house not a hundred miles from here – and not just occasionally, but every Thursday. Every single Thursday, ladies

and gentlemen, scenes like this take place, incredible
though it may seem – and in your ignorance, you may
feel safe – but here, for those of you who have the
courage to face the plain, unvarnished truth – here it
is, shocking in its fearless realism!

*The Knitting Group has assembled during this speech
and, as the lights come up on the acting area, they sit
perfectly quietly, knitting with great intensity. Around,
there is evidence of tea having been partaken of. They
must be very careful to avoid overpointing the double
meanings, which are very simple ones; simplicity will
make them more effective. They are all dear old ladies.*

EMILY: Well, who wants to indulge in some more?

MILLICENT: Well, I wouldn't mind another cup of tea,
dear.

EMILY: Certainly, dear. And who's for more . . . cake?

WINIFRED: Oh, I can't resist another piece, but it's
wicked, dear, downright wicked!

EMILY: Oh, come!

WINIFRED: Yes, wicked. I'm supposed to be on a diet
– but, alas, I simply can't resist temptation!

AMANDA: No woman ever has been able to – not since
Eve.

EMILY: Really, dear! Such frankness.

AMANDA: I believe in frankness. After all, we're emanci-
pated, we should be able to cast aside our restricting
inhibitions.

MILLICENT: Within limits, dear.

AMANDA: No, there should be no limits.

WINIFRED: Poor Amanda. She always was a bit ad-
vanced. I fear she'll be getting us a certain Reputa-
tion.

MAUD: Nevertheless, we must maintain our friendship with her – or I feel she will feel . . . abandoned.

AMANDA: I *am* abandoned. And I don't care who knows it.

JANE (*breaking up an awkward moment; greeting a newcomer*): Why, here comes Victoria! How nice to see you! I was so sorry when you turned aside from the path.

VICTORIA: No one could have regretted it more than I, my dear. But, believe me, never again will I turn aside from the path. The grass is so muddy.

EMILY: But what has held you back, dear?

VICTORIA: Oh, I've been assisting the Police with their inquiries.

EMILY: Oh, Victoria, how tiresome.

VICTORIA: Yes, they *still* haven't found the owner of that stray dog. I suppose it's too late for a drop of your potent brew.

EMILY: I'll make some fresh. I always say, when it comes to tea, you can't be too fresh.

VICTORIA: No, please, not just for me. It won't be all that long before we're off again.

EMILY: Oh, not for another half an hour at least.

VICTORIA: Half an hour? Oh, my dear, I'm fast! I'm terribly fast!

EMILY: You certainly are.

VICTORIA: Oh, by the way, I've just had a Sensational Offer!

MAUD: My dear, how exciting! Do tell us all!

VICTORIA (*producing knitting-needles*): These.

WINIFRED: Knitting-needles! But we've got knitting-needles!

VICTORIA: Ah, but these are special ones, the man said. Specially activated, or something. Apparently, they produce Sensational Results – the Experience of a Lifetime, he said. Anyway, I said we'd give them a try, at any rate.

AMANDA: By all means. Try anything once.

VICTORIA is giving out knitting-needles to the rest of the group. They slowly become affected; minor twitches, odd gleams. The effect builds up.

EMILY (*at the tea pot*): I'm afraid it's a bit stewed. Are you sure you wouldn't rather have some fresh?

VICTORIA (*in a strange voice*): No . . . if you don't mind, I'd rather have a cup of . . . hemlock . . . or better still, a flagon of . . . bat's blood!

They all begin to clamour for hemlock and bat's blood; twitching has now begun to develop into an embryonic Witches' Dance.

EMILY: Goodness gracious, this really is a Sensational Occurrence in Secluded Tilgate Close. If the *Observer* ever got hold of this! I know – it's all to do with those knitting-needles!

They all begin to intone 'Knitting-Needles!', intermingled with insane cackles.

EMILY: Give me those! (*She grabs some of the needles.*) I won't stand by while an innocent knitting-circle develops into a Witches' Sabbath! I won't stand by! . . . (*Becoming affected like the others.*) No, I'll join in!

To depraved chants of 'Knitting-Needles!', they cavort the acting area and leap off. Lights go down, except on the CHAIRMAN. He holds a copy of the local newspaper, from which he reads. Meanwhile, the setting is changed.

CHAIRMAN: 'An interesting addition to Crawley's varied social life is the newly formed Knitting and Orgy Group. Meetings are held in Tilgate Woods, monthly, according to the state of the moon. Intending members are required to supply their own hemlock, bat's blood – and, of course, knitting.' You see, they *did* get hold of it. They don't miss much. To the woods!

From the back of the hall, we hear GRAHAM's *voice echoing,* 'To the Woods!'. *The Gang surges on to the acting area, but the light comes up on the 'stage', revealing the* KNITTERS *grouped tastefully as if for the beginning of* 'Les Sylphides'. *The music starts gently and they dance, sedately.*

GRAHAM: Thank heavens! Providence has been benign. All is not lost.

Whereupon the VILLAIN *appears.*

VILLAIN. We can't have this! What revolution ever got going to the strains of Chopin? Forward the Philharmonic! Do your stuff! Let's have a bit of decadence round here!

Whereupon, we get a dose of Wagner. The strain of 'The Ride of the Valkyries' *echoes around. The* KNITTERS *leap into action, more and more witch-like.*

LUX: Foiled again! Amazing how potent bad music is.

The dance develops, wilder and wilder. MILDRED *goes up to them.*

MILDRED: Stop this disgraceful exhibition at once!

GRAHAM: Mildred! Keep away from them – there's

no knowing what they'll do, in their depraved and maddened state!

Whereupon, the WITCHES *grab hold of Mildred, and sweep off, followed by the* VILLAIN.

KEITH. The diabolical fiends! They've got Mildred!

WILLIAM: Well, I only hope they know what they've taken on.

GRAHAM: Just think – Mildred alone – in that fiendish mob!

WILLIAM: At least it'll be company for her.

LUX: But what shall we do?

GRAHAM: How . . . how can we rescue her from their inhuman clutches?

ROBERT: What dark fate awaits that frail child, held in thrall by the powers of darkness?

LUX: We must act. And act resolutely. Like true Englishmen.

Patriotic music. Solemn tableau.

GRAHAM: Well, then, men, what do you propose that we should do?

PHIL: I'm thirsty. How about having an interval?

KEITH: And abandon Mildred to her fate?

PHIL: Well, only for ten minutes or so.

The others all concur.

ROBERT: Still . . . poor, unhappy Mildred!

WILLIAM: Poor witches. (*As they start to go off, he turns to the audience.*) You can have an interval, too, if you like. (*He gives the details, half-turns to go then turns back.*) . . . Oh, and I shouldn't waste your interval worrying over-much about Mildred. If you knew the producer as well as I do, you'd realize that he wouldn't dream of killing off a

character during the interval. Not if he can squeeze
a few more laughs out of her. No such luck. Off
you go.
   The lights fade.

                    INTERVAL

ACT TWO

Ominous music. Spotlight on the CHAIRMAN. *He speaks in dire warning tones.*

CHAIRMAN: Crawley, your days are numbered. Nay, your very hours, your minutes. Light-heartedly, you frolic in the sun, queue for buses, look in the shop windows for bargains, settle before the familiar schedule of television, but I warn you: the sun will darken, the buses will no longer roll their tardy bulk along the road towards you; the shop windows will be empty, only the remains of stickers on the windows flapping in the breeze: 'Sensational Event', but sensation is past; 'Special This Week', but nothing special remains – or 'Hurry Before this Offer Closes', but all offers will have closed and no amount of hurrying will open them again. And, as for the familiar schedule of television, the time will shortly be upon you when the eye that glimmers in the corner of the room will be as void and lack-lustre as the eyes which gaze upon it. (*The mood of the music lightens a little.*) The trouble is, you just don't believe me, do you? Well, go ahead, admit it. You already have a fair indication of this man's incredible villainy. We've shown you, haven't we? Given you the full, unexpurgated story. Exclusive to this performance. What more do you want,

you disbelieving lot? (*Music builds up again.*) It's true,
I tell you, true – Disaster! Desolation! The lot! It's
on its way – any minute now – I've told you once, I'll
tell you again – *LISTEN*, will you! . . . (*A pause,
then, in a normal voice.*) You're quite right, of course.
It's no business of mine. My job is to introduce the
second part of this incomparable show, to reveal to
you the glittering wonders we have in store for you –
colour, excitement, glamour, heart-warming scenes
and dazzling moments that will make you hold
your breath! And, to commence: light-heartedly,
Crawley frolics in the sun, unaware of the doom
which is about to overtake it. Heedless of the threat to
their existence, the inhabitants pass the time in their
normal, feckless way, dancing the Queen's Square
Gavotte.

*This is really the opening chorus for the second part.
The inhabitants dance a take-off of a Gavotte done by
shoppers in a Supermarket. When they have moved off,
two suspiciously large babies, HERBERT and PERCY, are
wheeled on by their respective nursemaids, MABEL and
ELVIRA. This is a deliberate burlesque: the babies should
be obviously large and gruff. Nearby, an ice-cream van,
run by an Italianate ALFONSO.*

MABEL (*cooing*): There now, Herbert! There's a lovely
spot! See the fountain! Isn't it pretty, then?

HERBERT: Goo, goo.

MABEL: Oh, it's *so* pretty!

HERBERT: Goo!

ELVIRA (*also settling*): Who's a lucky boy, then – look
at the pretty fountain!

PERCY: Ga, ga, ga.

ELVIRA: There's a love! He almost talks, bless his little cotton socks!

PERCY (*joyful*): Ga, ga, ga!

ELVIRA: What does 'oo say, then?

PERCY: Booble, booble, booble.

ELVIRA: Does he like the pretty fountain, then?

PERCY: Ga.

ELVIRA: He does, the poppet!

MABEL: And does *oo* like the pretty fountain, then?

HERBERT: Goo.

MABEL: Oh, he does, oh, he's a gorgeous little pussi-kins – and he *loves* the pretty fountain, then.

HERBERT (*carried away*): Goo, goo, goo, goo, goo, goo, goo.

MABEL: Well then, 'oo shall have an ice-cream, 'oo shall. Who's a lucky boy, then?

HERBERT (*smug*): Goo.

MABEL: That's right, you clever little noddikins. Nursey will just go and get her little duckling a booful, scrum-shus ice-cream!

She moves off to the ice-cream van.

PERCY (*meaningful*): Ga, ga, ga.

ELVIRA: What is it, my precious?

PERCY: Ga, ga.

ELVIRA: What's the matter, then?

PERCY (*impatient*): Ga, ga!

ELVIRA: Oh, he wants an ice-cream?

PERCY: Glug.

ELVIRA: Not yet, my little honey-lamb. Wouldn't be good for um's little tummy-wum.

PERCY (*firmly*): Glug, glug, glug.

ELVIRA: Later on, perhaps, precious one.

PERCY *makes a great wail.*

ELVIRA (*peeved*): Oh very well then, Nursey's little ray of sunshine. And if it makes you sick, don't ask me to mop you up.

Both the NURSEMAIDS *are at the ice-cream van. The babies eye each other.*

PERCY (*tentative*): Hello.

HERBERT (*aggressive*): I'll bash you.

PERCY: Just you try.

HERBERT: All right, then.

He thumps Percy sharply with his rattle. A pause. PERCY *eyes him as he smiles smugly. Sharply, Percy belts him with a rubber duck. Another pause, then* HERBERT *slings a ball at Percy, with marked effect. Another pause.* PERCY *produces a cricket bat and thumps Herbert's pram also with marked effect. The fight escalates. At this point, the* NURSEMAIDS *return.*

ELVIRA: Oh look – they've been playing together!

MABEL: How sweet! They've been exchanging toys!

ELVIRA: Oh Percy, you little saucepot! Mustn't take other little boys' toys!

PERCY (*a bit sour*): Ga!

ELVIRA (*giving the toy back to Herbert*): There you are – what a kind little boy it is, then.

HERBERT (*smug*): Goo! Goo!

PERCY (*very sour*): Ga.

MABEL: Now then, noddykins – you just enjoy your booful ice-cream! Not too quickly, mind! (*As* HERBERT *settles to his ice-cream, she turns aside.*) Little do they know that I am really Secret Agent Number Thirty-Six, disguised with amazing ingenuity as a simple nursemaid. And my handbag is in fact a marvel of modern electronic ingenuity for receiving, monitoring, transmitting – and for converting pounds, shillings and pence into Decimal Currency.

ELVIRA: Now, don't forget, um is not to be sick, not till Nursey's off duty. (*Aside.*) And how surprised they would be to see me off duty, for I am really glamorous, tantalizing, exotic Secret Agent Number Thirty-Four. And my compact is absolutely the latest thing in electronics – open to transmit, closed to receive. (*She demonstrates; a blast of Radio One; she frowns and adjusts the set, receives Morse, smiles contentedly.*)

PERCY: Goo? Goo? . . . She's away. For a moment, I can relax from my tedious and unflattering pose. For little do they know that in fact I am really devil-may-care Agent Thirty-Seven and this, which appears to be a simple rattle, is, in fact, a transmitter of fantastic power. See: (*He pretends to switch it on.* ELVIRA *jumps a mile.*)

ELVIRA: Ohh! (*Apologetic, excusing.*) Indigestion . . . Pardon.

HERBERT: Time to tune in. Little do they know that *I* am steady, unimaginative Agent Thirty-Five. (*Modestly reticent.*) It's just another job, really. Well, aerial up . . . (*He puts up a toy 'windmill'.*) V.H.F. fitted . . . (*He adds a balloon.*) Receiver in place . . .

He holds the ball to his ear, then becomes aware that PERCY *is watching a bit dubiously, holding his rattle. To distract his attention, he says.*

HERBERT: Pwetty wattle!

PERCY: Yes, pwetty wattle!

This booms out through the 'ball', the 'handbag' and the 'compact'. General astonishment.

PERCY: Curses! Me cover's blown!

ELVIRA: 'Pwetty wattle!' That's not in the code book. There can only be one explanation! My secret has been discovered!

MABEL: All is lost! I have received an unexplained transmission!

HERBERT: I'm not a very bright person, but I reckon there's something very involved happening round here. And I think it's just possible that someone may have realized – goodness only knows how – that I am not in fact an unusually large infant, but actually steady, unimaginative Agent Thirty-Five.

PERCY: I heard that! You didn't say it sufficiently aside. And all is indeed discovered. For I am Agent Thirty-Seven.

MABEL: Agent Thirty-Seven! But I am Agent Thirty-Six!

ELVIRA: And I – I am Agent Thirty-Four!

HERBERT: That's very odd. Somehow . . . it seems to me . . . that we – go together – I'm not quite sure how, though . . .

ELVIRA: Wait a minute! Thirty-Four . . .

HERBERT: Thirty-Five!

MABEL: Thirty-Six!!

PERCY: Thirty-Seven!!!

ELVIRA: Well, we may not be a set, but we're certainly a sequence.

HERBERT: That's it! Astounding!

MABEL: Well, dear, now there's no longer any need for secrecy, I've been just dying to show someone this enchanting little handbag.

ELVIRA: Oh my dear, how sweet!

They enthuse over it. Meanwhile, PERCY *has been pondering.*

PERCY: Just one thing that's worrying me, Thirty-Five. If we've all been watching one another – do you think there's any possibility that anyone could – by any remote chance – have been watching . . . us?

The ICE-CREAM MAN *nonchalantly runs up the aerial on his cart, takes an ice-cream cornet and speaks into it.*

ALFONSO: Testing, testing, one two three, testing.

HERBERT *and* PERCY *look at each other, dubiously. Meanwhile.*

ELVIRA: But you haven't seen my enchanting little compact!

MABEL: Oh my dear, how sweet!

They start to move out.

PERCY: Hey! Wait a minute! Aren't you going to push us?

ELVIRA: Where's the point – now?

MABEL: Push yourselves!

They go off. PERCY *and* HERBERT *sit a moment, looking at each other, then.*

PERCY: I mean, one feels such a fool.

And they reluctantly get out of their prams, pushing them off the stage.

ALFONSO: Little do they know that every word has been observed, and will shortly be transmitted to the anti-Villain headquarters, where they are labouring night and day in a ceaseless vigil to combat World Revolution!

But the second ice-cream lid opens and a HEAD *pops out.*

HEAD: Little does he know that I've sabotaged his power supply.

He clambers out, following ALFONSO *off with elaborate precaution, turning as he goes out.*

HEAD: And I alone of this collection have been clever enough to escape unobserved. No one follows me. But no one.

But, as he exits, the HORSE *gallops on, pauses long enough to give a neighing laugh and wave a Union Jack, then gallops off after him. Lights down except for a spotlight on the* CHAIRMAN.

CHAIRMAN: And now, ladies and gentlemen, the moment for which I know many of you have been waiting: the next instalment of our thrilling serial 'The Perils of Mildred' brought to you with incredible verisimilitude by the modern miracle of Kinematography. You will no doubt recall that, at the end of the last episode, our frail heroine was left by the unspeakable villain, tied to the track of the London, Brighton and South Coast Railway, along which, at any moment, a locomotive was due to appear. I know that you are waiting breathlessly to discover: what will be the unhappy maiden's fate? Will the train run her over? Indeed, will the train run at all? Will the hero and his gallant band save her from a fate worse than closure? What will happen?

At this point, the Gang start to gather in the acting area. Light goes out quickly on the CHAIRMAN *and comes up on the acting area.*

GRAHAM: No sign.

ROBERT: No sign.

WILLIAM: I've searched *every*where.

LUX: Liar.

WILLIAM: Who are you calling a liar?

LUX: Someone I saw leaning up against a wall and stuffing himself with ice-cream.

WILLIAM: Well, I was tempted. I thought of a nice, cool, refreshing ice-cream, and then of hot, sticky, unappetizing Mildred and I just thought it was possible to sacrifice too much in the cause of chivalry.

PHIL (*arriving*): No sign.

KEITH (*arriving*): No sign.

WILLIAM: Well, I bet that's the last we'll ever see her.

GRAHAM: No, no. We must never give up. Remember the spirit of the Empire-builders. Remember, too, that we have inherited that birth-right. We must be British Bulldogs, never ceasing in our efforts, never relaxing our vigilance. Think, men, what this means – this fine flower of British womanhood, plucked away from us by this dastardly rotter; this frail blossom, wilting in his rapacious hands – ah, never let it be said —

Whereupon, the HORSE *enters.*

LUX: Look, a horse!

The HORSE *pushes* WILLIAM *in an attempt to get him off the side of the stage.*

WILLIAM (*peeved*); Here, here. You watch who you're pushing, mate. Don't try coming the old police horse act with me.

GRAHAM: He looks as if he's trying to get you to go with him.

WILLIAM: Well, he's got another think coming. My mum told me never to go with strange horses . . . stop *pushing*, will you?

PHIL: It's all a bit like 'Rescued by Rover' – you know,

the old films, where the faithful pet leads you to the heroine – ridiculous, those old films, weren't they?

KEITH: Oh, I don't know – I think they're rather exciting – you know, where the heroine's tied to the railway tracks —

The HORSE *performs some amazing convolutions.*

GRAHAM: Say that again!

KEITH: Say what?

GRAHAM: That bit about the heroine being tied to the railway tracks —

The HORSE *again shows great excitement.*

KEITH: I don't know what you're talking about.

ROBERT: You know, all about the heroine being tied to —

KEITH: Oh yes! You mean where the villain abducts the heroine and ties her to the railway tracks, and then the faithful pet comes along and somehow attracts the attention of the gallant hero, and . . . I say!

They look at the cavorting HORSE *with interest.*

LUX: You know, I believe there's some deep and unrevealed significance in all this. You don't think —

PHIL: No, no – it's not possible —

WILLIAM: On the other hand, it's my considered opinion that that horse is behaving uncharacteristically.

GRAHAM (*continuing the very serious and measured tone of the debate*): But in the films, it's always a dog!

LUX: Not in a Western, it isn't.

GRAHAM: That's true, they do use horses for the spectacular rescues in Westerns.

WILLIAM: Not all Westerns.

GRAHAM: No, no – I grant you that – not *all* Westerns. But some.

D

WILLIAM: Yes, some. I grant you that.

LUX: And Mildred *is* in desperate peril.

GRAHAM: Oh yes, utterly desperate. But, somehow, a horse . . .

KEITH: And if it could be a dog, then it could equally well be a horse —

PHIL: Oh surely not – I mean, after all, a dog is so much more intelligent than a horse.

KEITH: True, true. A dog is man's best friend.

WILLIAM: No, that's a horse, surely —

GRAHAM: You think so?

WILLIAM (*doubtful*): Yes, I *think* so —

GRAHAM (*almost convinced*): Oh well, in that case —

LUX: And Mildred *is* in desperate peril —

GRAHAM: Oh yes, utterly desperate —

LUX: So we should leave no stone unturned to find her.

GRAHAM: Unfortunately put, but I see what you mean. (*Solemn music.*) Very well, men – this simple creature of nature, this noble beast may be offering us a clue as to the whereabouts of Mildred. He may, on the other hand, be about to make us look very foolish indeed. However, we are Englishmen, and it is well known that no Englishman ever minds looking foolish, so long as it is in a good cause. So, I propose that we follow him in the hope that he may lead us to Mildred who, after all, is in utterly desperate peril – indeed, by this time, probably in extremis. Men – follow that horse!

A roll of drums. They turn, ready to rush off, but the HORSE *settles placidly and seems disinclined to move.*

PHIL (*peeved*): Well, how do you explain that, then?

One minute he's all anxious to get started and the next, he's stopped for no reason at all.

KEITH: Perhaps he's a Union horse.

PHIL: Perhaps someone's nobbled him – I know – try a bit of hurry music! (*The music starts and the* HORSE *comes smartly to life.*) There you are – he was just waiting for his cue. Follow that horse!

ALL: To the ends of the earth if necessary! Follow that horse!

They charge off. Hurry music continues. Lights come up on the 'stage' and the Gang, the VILLAIN *and the* HORSE *enact a silent film sequence. If the lights flicker, this helps. A basic plot is: The* VILLAIN *drags on* MILDRED; *she mimes screaming and distraction. He mimes tying her to the rails and lurks off, twirling his moustache. On comes the* HORSE, *then the Gang. They start to untie* MILDRED, *but at that moment the* VILLAIN *appears, propelling a cut-out train.* KEITH *holds this off with one hand, but a great appearance of effort. The Gang release* MILDRED *and charge off, with the* VILLAIN *pursuing them, shaking his fist. This should all be done in fast, jerky movement. The lights go down on the 'stage' and the* VILLAIN *reappears in the acting area.*

VILLAIN: Curses! foiled for the first time. Ah well, I suppose being foiled is all part of a villain's lot; you can't be a fully-fledged, dyed-in-the-wool bounder without a bit of foiling – and what does it matter, anyway – it would just have been an entertaining diversion, but what matters an unmashed Mildred when considered against the massive and ingenious piece of devilry which I am about to launch. Ha ha!

Fortunately I am unobserved, for I cannot restrain myself from the pleasure of an audible gloat.

At which point the Gang enter. They pause on seeing the Villain.

GRAHAM: Cautiously now, men – and Mildred. He must not know that he is observed. Conceal yourselves behind this bush and no doubt we shall hear something to our disadvantage.

They all gather behind an absurdly small bush, from which they emerge fully to make their various comments. The VILLAIN *has not noticed their arrival: continuing, oblivious.*

VILLAIN: Aha! I am about to launch my wickedness in precisely that area where there is without doubt the greatest scope for ingeniously directed villainy – the world of salesmanship; surely there can be no aspect of that world better suited to the calculated deployment of skilful devilment than that of high-powered advertising ... oh bless my soul (if I may use such an inappropriate phrase) I can hardly contain my fiendish chuckles or my chameleon-like changes of countenance.

He chuckles and changes colour remarkably. WILLIAM *emerges, unheard by him.*

WILLIAM: Oh heavens, what new devilment is here revealed? Can it be that this thrice-blackened cur really plans to strike at the hallowed preserves of commerce and public relations! Woe is us!

MILDRED: Be not faint-hearted, have no fear, for in this dastardly scheme, he has at last over-reached himself, for there are limits, yes, even to the justly famed tolerance of the Englishman.

GRAHAM: True, true. An Englishman will tolerate the odd orgy: yes, even the tying of a female to the railway lines – provided, that is, that it does not interfere unduly with the scheduled timetable, but an Englishman's advert is his fantasy – and woe betide the person who attempts to interfere with an Englishman's fantasies!

LUX: But hush, and we may perchance overhear what he intends to do.

VILLAIN: This, then, I intend to do. My minions are even now preparing to mount a series of promotions in that throbbing heart of commercial life, Queen's Square. And – hee, hee, hee! The housewives, poor simple creatures, will succumb to their fiendish blandishments, I am sure of it.

KEITH: Gracious heavens! The man's an unmitigated bounder!

LUX: But hush, and he may reveal more.

VILLAIN: Nay, I will reveal more – for when those poor, deluded creatures hasten to buy the spurious articles which my minions will cunningly persuade them to purchase – little will they know – nay, little will anyone know – that, when the cash registers reach a certain figure – hee, hee, hee – BOOM!

MILDRED: Sakes alive! What can he mean?

ROBERT: Alas, that is too plain, I fear.

LUX: But hush, and there may be more to come.

VILLAIN: And there is more to come. At the moment of the explosion, I will release the cunningly concealed hordes of one of my allies, who has an aversion to consumer goods on principle. The distracted dupes will be driven remorselessly to the woods, there to

be overcome by another means that I will gloat
about later, for this gloat has been quite enough to
outline the immediate situation. To Queen's Square!

GANG: To Queen's Square!

The VILLAIN *pauses, ponders, then decides.*

VILLAIN: Echo.

And goes out. The Gang come out of 'concealment'.

PHIL: He'll never get away with this!

ROBERT: I'm not so sure – I mean, in other respects,
like messing about with the railways, he's been playing with fire, but it seems to me that when it comes to
advertising, however much you mess about, you're
fire-proof.

PHIL: Right, that's enough talk for the time being –
from now on, let's have lots and lots of action. Posters
first, then to Queen's Square!

GANG (*a solemn procession, to a strong rhythmic support*):
Posters first, posters first, then Queen's Square!

*They build this up, marching round the 'stage', then
go out. The 'stage' is lit, and the acting area fills with
buyers. The scene develops freely as a piece of improvised
crowd work, then the first of the* ADVERTISERS *jumps on
to the 'stage' and draws their attention. The following are
suggestions for advertisements, but the cast could well
supply much better ones themselves.*

ADVERTISER: Ladies and gentlemen! Do you feel you're
missing out in life? Feel the need for something that's
a bit different? NEW – scientifically developed – now
available to all, the new, exciting, new, unusual, new,
all-purpose medium – *MUD*!

An OLD LADY *bounces on.*

OLD LADY (*brightly*): I just love throwing mud! How

it sticks! It's such fun! Try some new MUD on your
neighbour today – it makes such a difference to life!

She is replaced by a BABY, *who lisps very articulately.*

BABY: What lovelier sound is there in life than the
gurgle of a baby brought up on MUD? I eat lots of
things, worms, spiders, bits of coal – but my favourite
is . . . MUD!

The BABY *is pushed off and a Skinhead appears. He
intones.*

SKINHEAD: There's nothing like MUD for starting an
agro. I find it by far the most effective medium for
plastering the opposing football team. Next time
you're stuck for a bit of fun – think of me – and remember, the name is MUD!

The ADVERTISER *intervenes.*

ADVERTISER: And, what's more, it's in the shops *now*!
New MUD – sixpence off. Go, give yourself a treat –
get down to some MUD today!

The SHOPPERS *are immediately overcome by the need
for MUD. With shrill screams, they rush off to the store to
buy their Mud, undeterred by the Gang, who march
round with large posters saying 'Don't stop at Tesworths'
and so on. The cash registers ring and ring. Then, another*
ADVERTISER *leaps on to the 'stage' to attract the shoppers'
attention.*

ADVERTISER: Ladies and gentlemen, you've not heard
anything yet!

A DOCTOR *appears: a very medical manner.*

DOCTOR: Or, put it another way: you've heard too
much. It's one of the problems of our everyday life –
noise!

A MOTHER *and her* CHILDREN *are seen – radio blaring,*

children banging, screaming, all sorts of extraneous noise. As it builds to a crescendo, she puts her hands to her ears and screams. But the scream is soundless and, simultaneously, all other noises stop.

DOCTOR: Notice the difference? She's discovered G.T.Z.3, commonly known as SILENCE. We scienitsts have toiled for years to isolate this precious ingredient and at last we have succeeded. Here it is . . . (*he holds up a bottle of green liquid*) *new* – G.T.Z.3 – you call it . . . (*There is no sound; he mouths 'silence'.*)

ADVERTISER: *Now* in the shops – for you – new (*he mouths 'silence'*) . . . sixpence off!

Again, despite the efforts of the Gang, the SHOPPERS *rush off to the shop to buy. A crescendo of till bells, building up and up – then a huge explosion. The* SHOPPERS *rush, screaming, out of the shop, only to meet an evil horde of* CHINESE, *who chase them off in another direction. The* CHINESE *then form up and, to the tune of 'Chopsticks', perform a shuffly sort of dance, with a lot of bowing to and fro, announced as:*

CHINAMAN: Now we dance fiendish Oriental Dance of Diabolical Tliumph.

At the end of their dance, the last two suddenly turn, rush towards Mildred and carry her off before the Gang can intervene. They exit, chuckling wickedly.

KEITH: The diabolical fiends! They've got Mildred, too!

WILLIAM: Well I don't know, it's a bit much really, the way Mildred keeps letting herself get carried away.

GRAHAM: Oh come now, men – ours not to reason why, you know.

WILLIAM: Well I don't know so much. I think it's carrying dramatic licence a bit far.

ROBERT: Courage, friend, we cannot back down now. However distasteful it may seem, we must unquestioningly accept the White Man's burden.

WILLIAM: Meaning Mildred?

ROBERT: Meaning Mildred.

WILLIAM: Oh very well, but it gets a bit tedious, I don't mind telling you. I find it extremely difficult to work up any real enthusiasm for the clarion cry: to the woods!

Music – but it is extremely lethargic. PHIL *addresses the musicians.*

PHIL: Is that the tempo to take? Don't you realize that if we don't hurry, Mildred may finish up having her throat cut.

Whereupon the music slows down and stops altogether.

PHIL: Oh well, if that's your attitude, we'll have to employ the other firm!

Recorded music – the 'Ride of the Valkyrie', starting very slowly, at 16 r.p.m., then changing to 33, then 45, then 78. Their movements brisken correspondingly, and they shoot off to a gabble of sound. Lights on the CHAIRMAN, *off the rest of the area.*

CHAIRMAN: The next scene, like all the preceding ones, is unfit for people with weak nerves. We move once again to darkest Tilgate Forest, haunt of coot, fern and variegated humankind, the very trunks and branches acquiver with doom. Step from the path and you are drawn irresistibly into evil quicksands; pause by the lake – a tentacle appears and hideously sucks you under till nothing remains but bubbles breaking on the surface; walk unwarily and you disappear for ever into an elephant trap. Truly, no one but a brave man – or a fool – would set foot in this forest without desperate cause. And yet, our intrepid band are at this very moment advancing fearlessly towards the forest with no thought of personal danger or of the dread perils which await them. . . .

Light goes off from him, comes up on the acting area. The setting has been changed. The Gang creep on to the acting area, not very bravely. GRAHAM *halts them.*

GRAHAM: Not so fast, men! There's something devilish odd going on. I feel it in me bones.

LUX: How – odd?

GRAHAM: Deuce take it, I can't tell. But it's too quiet for my liking. Far too quiet. It's not healthy, men.

KEITH: How about going back for reinforcements?

WILLIAM: And leave Mildred in their fiendish clutches?

KEITH: Well, I don't think it would make all that difference if they gave her a few minutes' extra clutch.

ROBERT: Hark!

The sound of galloping hooves is heard.

LUX: That's never Mildred!

The HORSE *gallops across the stage and disappears rapidly.*

WILLIAM: It's a horse!

LUX: It's *the* horse!

PHIL: Are you sure?

LUX: There can't be another like that, surely! But why is it galloping away like that?

An arrow whizzes across the stage, following the horse. ROBERT *walks and picks it up.*

ROBERT: Now that's very strange. Archery Club's on Wednesdays.

GRAHAM: There's something mighty strange going on here.

LUX: But – an arrow! What could it signify?

ROBERT: Arrows only signify one thing in my reckoning —

KEITH: And what's that?

ROBERT: Injuns!

ALL (*derisive*): Injuns!

ROBERT: Well, there's only one way to find out —

He moves towards the side of the 'stage'.

GRAHAM: You fool! Don't you realize – that way lurks danger, unspeakable horror – nameless dread.

ROBERT: Let it lurk. Do not attempt to dissuade me, for it is a far, far better thing that I do now than I have ever done before.

To resounding music, he exits.

LUX: Stout fellow!

PHIL: Stout fellow, my foot! Of all the utterly incredible, totally impossible ideas! Injuns! I ask you! Vampires – yes, regularly; anacondas – naturally; man-eating tigers – abundantly; crocodiles – frequently; Dracula – inevitably. But I ask you – I *tell* you – what could possibly be more absurd than the very idea of . . .

A high, warbling noise from the forest; they crouch together in wide-eyed terror.

ALL (*a whisper*): Injuns!

WILLIAM: And that gallant fellow has gone to his doom. Ah, the pity of it! The desperate, heart-breaking sacrifice of it! Poor Robert! Poor . . . Robert!

This last is occasioned by ROBERT'S *entrance, scalped.*

ROBERT: So! You laughed me to scorn! But who laughs now? Eh? Who laughs now?

KEITH: But it *can't* be!

ROBERT: It *is*!

Warbling noises off.

ALL (*horror*): Injuns!

LUX: In my view, this whole thing is becoming just a bit too multi-racial.

ROBERT: *And* they've got Mildred!

KEITH: Say what you like, she does get around.

Noises off. ROBERT *receives a totem pole from the wings and places it in the centre of the area.*

ROBERT: Run, run for your lives – they are coming this way – possibly to make use of this totem pole, which I had hitherto not observed.

GRAHAM: Let us conceal ourselves. We cannot desert Mildred in her hour of greatest need. Here they come!

The Gang lurk to one side, where they are unobserved by the INJUNS *as they come on to tie Mildred to the stake, despite her violent struggles.*

CHIEF: Now um make heap good war-dance.

BRAVES: Ug!

CHIEF: And, to follow, we give pale-face mini-squaw heap good scalping.

BRAVES: But first, um make highly articulate song representing triumphant thoughts on taking over English woodland area in which to set up white man's reserve where Indian braves can visit preserved Englishmen and take heap good cine films of them in their natural habitat.

BRAVES: Ug, ug, ug!

CHIEF: Heap good articulate song to be accompanied by heap good ingenious and effective actions.

BRAVES: Ug, ug, ug!

The INJUNS *sing their Ug song. Each small group has its note, or notes, which they sing at appropriate times. As each group sings its note, it moves into a grouping, then relaxes, inert, till the note comes round again. More simply, the* INJUNS *can sing a well-known tune, using 'ug' as the only sound.*

CHIEF: Heap good song. Now, Indian braves make heap good war-dance, and then —

He moves close to Mildred, indicating fiendishly what he will do.

MILDRED: Ug!

The INJUNS *take up their positions and, to the accompaniment of percussion, start their war-dance. After a while, they pause, frozen into their positions, apparently unaware of the Gang's words and actions, except later on, where they produce various impatient Ug noises.*

LUX: Poor Mildred! What can we do?

ROBERT: What, indeed? They're a tricky lot, as I know to my cost.

KEITH: I have been visited by a brilliant idea!

PHIL: Then tell us quickly – and briefly – for soon it will be too late, and poor Mildred will be —

GRAHAM: Don't! I can't bear the thought of it – poor Mildred – hairless! Tell us your plan, however inept it may be.

KEITH (*pontificating*): This is a time for desperate measures.

WILLIAM: True.

KEITH: Indeed, it may well be said that a desperate situation calls for a desperate remedy.

WILLIAM: True.

KEITH: And if ever there was a desperate situation, this one is, truly . . . desperate.

ROBERT: Oh shut up and get on with it.

KEITH: Who are you telling to shut up and get on with it?

ROBERT: Who do you think?

KEITH: You want to watch it, mate.

ROBERT: So?

KEITH: I'm just telling you, that's all.

ROBERT: So?

KEITH: Right, then.

ROBERT: Right.

The mood is a reproduction of the earlier fight scene, and the same bubbling noise precipitates it. They swirl into a fight, egged on by the others and unobserved by the INJUNS. *At last,* LUX *pulls them apart, as before.*

GRAHAM: Hist! Fortunately, we are still unobserved. Make haste, tell us your desperate plan.

KEITH: This, then, is my desperate plan. I propose to insinuate myself into their primitive and impassioned dance – hoping that they will not notice such a civilized interloper – and to lead them, unsuspecting, into the lake, where they will all drown. That is my desperate plan.

WILLIAM: Gad, an ingeniously desperate plan! But will it work?

KEITH: It must, if we are to save Mildred.

LUX: Then it must be tried, no matter how desperate it may be.

ALL: Agreed! Agreed!

ROBERT (*a manly clasp of the hand*): Then, to it! Heaven knows, we have sparred enough in the past, yet now I cannot forbear to shed a tear, albeit a manly one – may good fortune go with you on your desperate mission. Farewell, my brave little companion, and if you do not return —

CHIEF (*impatient*): Ug!

KEITH: If I do not return, keep this as a memento of me. And when you look upon it, think, if you will, of your erstwhile friend —

CHIEF (*warning*): Ug!

KEITH: Who has sacrificed his life for an ideal and fought his last fight – alone.

GANG: Ug!

KEITH: Who shares a watery grave with those who sought to destroy all that was precious in life for him —

GANG *and* INJUNS: Ug!

　KEITH *detaches himself from the Gang. The war dance starts up again. Keith then insinuates himself into the circle and leads them off; they follow him unthinkingly* WILLIAM *goes to look as the others release Mildred.*

MILDRED (*nagging*): Well, you took your time, didn't you? I suppose you think I enjoyed being stuck here, tied to this ridiculous pole while you went all heroic over my predicament. Men! I ask you!

GRAHAM (*peeved*): Well, there's gratitude for you!

MILDRED: Gratitude! What have I got to be grateful for – I mean, I ask you – there you were – *lurking*, and doing nothing but talk. I mean, how would you like to be surrounded by that deafening yodelling,

enough to split your ear-drums, and, as if *that* wasn't
enough —

ROBERT: Hey, William, call those Injuns back, for
goodness' sake!

WILLIAM: Too late!

Screams, splashes and gurgling noises off. WILLIAM
staggers back, much moved.

WILLIAM: Ah, horrible, horrible!

PHIL: Really?

WILLIAM: Too horrible to relate! Ah, lackaday!

LUX: All . . . drowned?

WILLIAM: Worse, worse, far worse!

GRAHAM: Worse than drowning? What can you mean?

WILLIAM: All nicked by the Warden for illicit bathing.

LUX: Egad, a desperate end! And . . . Keith?

WILLIAM: Paused, trembling, on the very brink!

LUX: A true Englishman!

WILLIAM: Let us go and pay tribute to him – even
though his sacrifice is sadly unappreciated in certain
spheres.

MILDRED: Unappreciated! I like that! He didn't even
get his feet wet, did he? Sacrifice, indeed! I think it's
about time someone saw this whole masculine hoax
in perspective!

GRAHAM: Enough! Enough! Babbling female, how dare
you cast aspersions on the sacred, immutable law of
masculine superiority! I warn you, you go too far.

*As she speaks, they start to creep away; she continues,
oblivious.*

MILDRED: When I *think* of all I've put up with, and the
generous, good-humoured tolerance I've displayed –
and when I compare it with your rude, boorish,

arrogance, your complete disregard of … they've gone!
How extremely irritating, as I had a great deal more
to say, in similar vein.

   The VILLAIN *lurches on, upset. She rounds on him.*

MILDRED: And what do *you* want? Haven't you done
   enough lurking round for one day?

VILLAIN: My heart misgives me.

MILDRED: And so it jolly well should! I mean, look at
   it logically, you must know you're bound to come
   off worst in the end.

VILLAIN: Never!

MILDRED: Believe me, yes! We always do such *moral*
   plays, you just don't stand a chance.

VILLAIN: I won't listen!

MILDRED (*high minded*): No man is irredeemably wicked.

VILLAIN (*complacent*): I am.

MILDRED: Ah no, never let it be said —

VILLAIN: But it's true, I tell you, you idiot female. I'm
   a villain and that's that.

MILDRED: No, no, hearken to my words: there is hope
   for all. (*Music.*)

VILLAIN: Not for me, I tell. (*In a fury.*) And stop that
   ridiculous music! Look, you're a modern child, but
   I'm an old-fashioned villain. You were brought up
   on psychology and I was brought up on fire and
   brimstone. And we're both in a mess.

MILDRED: No, no, don't you *see*! If you had been a
   modern child, then you'd have been maladjusted
   or deprived or something like that – and that's so
   complicated putting you right would be an awful job.
   You'd have to be readjusted, or compensated, or
   something. Whereas you're simply an old-fashioned,

down-to-earth rotter. So with you, it's simple! All *you* have to do is to repent!

VILLAIN: Ah', how easily you say that – but my heart is blackened beyond repentance!

MILDRED: Never!

VILLAIN: *Will* you stop contradicting! It *is*, I tell you!

MILDRED: Ah, but think – think – once, it was not so. Once, you were an innocent little child, absorbed in childish pleasures.

VILLAIN: I pulled the wings off flies and stamped on little girls' toes.

MILDRED: But think! Reflect! Think of the innocence of childhood. See, see, how the children frolic in the sun!

Sentimental music: CHILDREN *trip in and play innocently.*

VILLAIN: Ah me! The simple innocence of children, playing in the sun! Ah, welladay! Something heaves within me – can it be repentance – or nausea?

CHILD (*coming up to him; glutinous sweetness*): See the pretty flower!

VILLAIN: What is this strange sensation? Can it be – ah heavens, can it be – repentance?

CHILD: *You* have the pretty flower – *you* is a *good* man!

VILLAIN: Ah, but an hour ago, I would have struck her to the ground, but now, this simple innocence moves me strangely.

2ND CHILD: Hold my dolly.

VILLAIN: Who? Me?

2ND CHILD: Yes, I trust you. You is a kind man.

VILLAIN (*gradually breaking into tears*): Never, I tell you – I am a wicked black-hearted, monstrous villain – nothing touches me, nothing moves me, nothing, nothing! (*He sobs noisily.*)

2ND CHILD: Why is you cwying?

VILLAIN: I weep for repentance, for my mis-spent youth. Ah, why could I not have spread goodness and happiness on my way through life? Ah, the bells, the bells of repentance ring within my ears!

MILDRED: But all is not too late.

VILLAIN: I fear – I fear it is.

MILDRED: No no! Let it not be said! Come, there is still time to undo the evil you have done.

VILLAIN: Can it be so?

MILDRED (*grimly*): It had better be so. No point in a last-minute repentance unless it sorts things out.

VILLAIN: My heart misgives me! I have left it perilously late, for even now, at my new secret headquarters, there is being held a special pre-massacre tea-dance. After that – the deluge.

MILDRED: Then hurry! Before it is too late!

VILLAIN: Yes, we must make haste. Could I ever allow these innocent heads to be laid low, these lisping voices to be silenced for ever? (*Thoughtfully.*) Could I? (*Remembering himself.*) No, no, it cannot be! It must not be! I am a new man, and the world shall know it. To the special pre-massacre tea-dance!

ALL: To the special pre-massacre tea dance!

Hurry music; they all hurry off. Light on the CHAIR-MAN. *The setting is changed.*

CHAIRMAN: And, for our grand finale, the entire cast will assemble to present a stirring last scene in which excitement blends with pathos, brilliance with simplicity, thrills with noble sentiments – and all these ingredients blended into a breath-taking scene of vivid vitality and vivacious virtuosity!

His light goes down; lights on the 'stage' and the acting area. A lot of wildly dressed people are assembled for the orgy. To strongly rhythmic music, preferably by a live group, they dance with increasing intensity. When the orgy is at its height, the VILLAIN *enters on the 'stage', and there is silence.*

VILLAIN: Stop! Stop! Oh, cannot you see, cannot you comprehend, the utter folly of this desperate wickedness. My friends, I have repented of my villainy, and I implore you to do likewise. I heeded nothing, nothing, in my black villainy, until my heart was touched – touched by a little child (*Sympathetic noises.*) who gave me – who gave me – a flower! (*More noises.*) And yet another who, tender and unafraid, gave me her little doll to hold – ah, the simple trustfulness of that gesture! It was that simple gesture, my friends, which touched my heart, and I resolved to lay aside my villainy for ever – and I beg you – nay, I implore you, to follow my example!

Great cries of 'We will! We will!' *Touching scenes of repentance.*

VILLAIN: Then it is not too late! Oh, my friends, how happy you have made me!

Whereupon, a group of fiendish Chinese rush on.

CHINAMAN: Not so fast! You still have us to contend with. And *we* are not so easily moved. We stand lesolute. Don't move. There is a machine-gun tlained on your wicked heart. One false move, and the last thing you will hear will be that gun's lattle.

Groans of horror.

VILLAIN: Curses! Foiled at me moment of repentance.
It's a bit much.

Cries of amazement as the HORSE *gallops in.*

HORSE: Not so fast. At last the time has come to reveal
ourselves. For we are not, in fact, a horse! (*Cries of
amazement as the two characters step from inside the
skin.*) But really, handsome, dynamic . . . (*name*) and
brilliant backroom boy . . . (*other name*).

General amazement.

CHINAMAN: Too late! One false move from you and
that villain dies.

HORSE: You gloat too soon. One false move from *you*
and we reveal to the world the full, secret and hitherto
unpublished story of Maisie Clophanger!

CHINAMAN: You wouldn't!

HORSE: We would – and what's more, we'd make a tidy
profit selling it to the newspapers. Be off with you,
and console yourself with your Thoughts.

The CHINESE *all gallop off. Cheers from the remaining
crowd.*

VILLAIN: Ah, there's nothing like a good, honest cheer,
emanating from good, honest English throats. Salute
these gallant specimens of English youth who braved
untold perils! (*The Gang enter proudly, to cheers.*)
Salute them in song; lift up your honest British voices
and join me in chorally declaiming:

They all sing 'There'll always be an England' *or
some other patriotic ballad. Patriotic Tableau. The play
ends.*